In the Garden

"For lo, the winter is past;

the rain is over and gone;

The flowers appear on the earth;

The time of singing is come."

In The Garden

By Kim Y. Jackson

In The Garden

Published by God's Glory Publishing Company, Inc.

ISBN 0-9743749-0-3

Cover designed by Shaina Victoria – Xtrardinaree Designs

Printing by Kinko's: Liana K. Jones Account Manager

Acknowledgments

To my Heavenly Father, be thou Glorified.

Bishop J. Charles Carrington, Jr. - I thank God for a shepherd tirelessly exhibiting his heart for God's people, and sincerely guiding them to fulfillment! 2nd Thessalonians 1:11

Thank God for your obedience Prophetess Diane Palmer-lead by the Lord-you spoke healing into my heart, and let me know in advance that my job would change. I never knew that writing for the Lord would be one of "many" new jobs God has blessed me with. Isaiah 55:11

To my son Ryan, the Praise Warrior. Thank you for sharing me with my "PC." You are such a blessing. Son, I thank God for being your mother. You have taught me a lot about God's unconditional love. I will forever remember your warmth and constant reminders to write. Than you for tolerating me in "The Garden." Jeremiah 1:4-10

To my "beautiful" daughter Tiffany. The beautiful flower God has placed in my life. May this book help you to come to the full knowledge of Christ. 2nd Peter 3:18

Sharon Ewell Foster, author of Passing by Samaria-your warm personable spirit, saw a burden in my heart to write, and encouraged me to do so. We really never know the impact of a brief encounter with another member of the body of Christ. God used you to help me break free. Phillipians 4:17

To my advisor, brother/prayer warrior for Christ, Dr. Steven A. Johnson, you are a blessing from God. Thanks for preaching Detours to your Destiny, and constantly reminding me through each trial "That I was still standing." May the abundant blessings from God saturate you for your obedience. Genesis 28:15

Presbyter Delores Golphin a very special thank you for unselfishly using your many gifts, talents and abilities. But most of all I thank God for your encouragement. The power that God has placed within you to lead His people in worship is awesome. I pray that you continue to lead His people behind the veil. Thank you for helping me to learn that "He will keep you in perfect peace whose mind is stayed on Him. May God Bless and Keep you always. Luke 18:27

To Rodney Bryant, Kurt Carr, and the Kurt Carr Singers. May God be Glorified with all your works. I thank God for your words of Praise to Him. Thank you for listening to the Holy Spirit to tell God's people, He put His trust in me to carry out His will. "That's just the way the Father is" inspired me to aspire to the Glory of God. 1st Corinthians 10:31

To all the Saints of God, especially my Zion Temple Fellowship Family. Thank you for your love, prayers, and support. I pray that you receive these words of Life from the Lord. 1ˢᵗ Corinthians 2:9

Sons and Daughters of God Arise! God Bless You.

In the Garden

"For lo, the winter is past;
the rain is over and gone;
The flowers appear on the earth;
The time of singing is come."

Song of Songs 2:11

Table of Contents

In the Garden

Introduction

"In the Garden" came through revelation from God while working in my own garden. The lot that God had given me to toil needed much work. Every step in the garden depicts the steps God orchestrated for my healing, deliverance, and transformation. God had a divine purposed for me to work in the garden, at the time he had appointed. I thought it was an opportunity to transform a plot of ground. But the transformation was really taking place in me. God wanted me to recognize that the life He had given me was not my own. He performed a miracle in me through the process of bring forth flowers in my garden. I pray that everyone who reads this book will seek the Lord to receive their own revelation.

"For as the earth brings forth its bud,
As the garden causes the things that are
Sown in it to spring forth,
So the Lord God will cause righteousness
And praise to spring forth before all the nations.

(Isaiah 61:11)

In the Garden

Chapter 1: Examine your lot

My lot, the place God ordained as my vineyard, was measured out and given to me according to God's will. The word of God found in Jeremiah 1:5 declares "Before I formed thee in the belly I knew thee; and before thou camest forth out of the womb I sanctified thee." Therefore, in God's magnificence, He set the stage for my total existence. As I embarked upon an endeavor to toil in a garden, God began to show me the need for him to conduct a spiritual gardening process in me. I thought it was about planting a garden. But it was really about the steps of preparation God had ordained for me to become a vessel He could use- for His Glory.

I began examining ground to begin planting. Upon careful examination I saw an area approximately 8' 1/2' x 11'. I wondered what I could possibly do with this ground that was filled with a variety of ground coverings. The lot needed to be thinned out, weeded back, cut down, replanted, and fertilized. Toiling in this lot for several weeks, I began to see that there was something special about to take place.

Definition

Lot is defined as a share of an estate or property. The Hebrew word Goral represents the "lot" which was cast to discover the will of God in a given situation, our fate, or destiny. At some time in our life we have to consider our lot or what is the divine will for our life.

In the Garden

Why does God give lots?

As a" babe" in Christ, I never completely considered, desired, prayed for or sought after God's will for my life. Though I now consider it daily, I wonder how much different my life would have been, had I daily considered - "His Will.". Regardless, God factored all of this into the equation for the fulfillment of my purpose, - which is to Glorify Him.

I must admit that I had difficulty accepting my lot. It was a journey filled with years of tears. But for every experience I had in my lot, God continuously assured me that He was with me. God gave me His Word that "The steps of a good man are ordered by the Lord."(Psalms 37:23)

My lot's Design

God designed my lot specifically to His dimensions. It has an exterior-the flesh; an interior, the Holy Spirit- dwelling within me; a working mechanism - the effective use of God's ordained time; value that increases continually- building up the body of Christ; and that which is extremely significant to the kingdom of God-one's purpose. The lot God gave me is unique. Even the vivid colors in my lot represent the intensity of God's magnificence, brilliance, and power. The depths of my lot are filled with challenges, pitfalls, mercy missions, and missions of weariness. Most of all, my lot continues to be filled with God's grace and mercy.

Included within the specific dimensions were designs for administration. My lot could not be functional without some, shall I say, reorganization. A major reorganization took place in my attitude, my belief in God's power, the words I spoke, and thoughts I allowed to consume my mind. A shift took place from self-centeredness to God centeredness, from the mind of man to the mind of Christ. The apostle Paul reminds us in Romans 12:2 "And do not be conformed to this world, but be transformed by the renewing of your mind." This shift brought forth a change in me that only God could perform. I needed this reconstruction so that God could complete what He had started in me. He did this so that the things He had apportioned for my estate would be effectively administrated for His Glory. God had gifts and treasures in my lot waiting to be released, that I would not be able to handle if my lot wasn't rearranged. What a wonderful God we serve!

Familiar lots

Some lots in our life are temporary assignments. The bible tells us in Genesis that two angels came to Sodom and Gomorrah, where they found Lot and instructed him to take his family and leave because of the preeminent destruction upon the city. The next morning Lot was not only told to leave again with his family, but was mercifully escorted outside of the walls of the city. Lot and his family were also told to escape with their lives, and not look back. Lot's wife looked back and turned to a pillar of salt. She, like many Christians, looked back to the past as a place of refuge (a comfort zone) because it was a familiar place. We have to be careful not to become comfortable with familiar lots. They may be places that we had been used to dwelling in, but they are not always the most fruitful.

Unfamiliar lots

God, in His sovereign way, coordinated my path to unfamiliar ground. I found that in order for me to access the place that God has destined for me I must have the faith to believe that as He orders my steps, I don't have to be anxious in my walk. Trusting God has been the key to moving forward in His grace, to my lot. Trust enabled me to walk when I felt that there was no evidence of His presence, though I knew that He promised, "I will never leave you nor forsake you." (Hebrews 13:5)

The Purpose of a lot

Like Lot's wife and family, I was directed by God to do some things that didn't appear reasonable. God's word declares, "But God has chosen the foolish things of the world to put to shame the wise." (1st Corinthians 1:27) God chose me to believe, accept, and take instructions from the Spirit of God, which I could not see. It had been ordained for this tie for Him to reveal himself. I thank God for His patience in guiding me through my "gardening process." When I didn't get things right, God mercifully came back, over and over, until I moved forward to the place He set aside for me to receive His blessings and fulfill my purpose.

My lot

My lot wasn't just the steps He had ordered for me to walk. I had to examine my walk and the character of Christ I was reflecting. Lot was obedient to God's direction. In this journey I had to earnestly evaluate my obedience to the Lord. I had to also evaluate my "self - will" better known as my "flesh". The Holy Spirit would often formulated questions in my mind like "Did I obey what thus saith the Lord? Did I ignore the Lord? Was I walking uprightly before Him? Did I desire to have the mind of Christ? Was I God centered? Did I have and was I exhibiting the Fruits of the Holy Spirit: Love, Joy,

In the Garden

Peace, Long Suffering, Kindness, Goodness, Faithfulness, Gentleness, and Self-Control? Was I faithful to the ministry God had given to me? Was I humble? Did I take direction from authority? What were my motives in helping people? Of course there are so many more questions. God has intricately used these questions as a means for me to evaluate my motives. For you the questions may not be the same. But, the questions still remains, "How do you answer your questions when the Holy Spirit shows you areas in your life that need to be changed"?

These questions came to remind me that if I couldn't answer yes or answer them in a way that reflected the spirit of Christ that God was going to initiate a process to reconfigure characteristics that were not like Him. I needed to be aware that God was going to shake these things up and off of me at all cost, so that He could use me to build His kingdom. I felt honored that He would use me to show forth His mighty works and that His people would praise Him for my purpose in His kingdom.

God's promise for our lots
The bible speaks of the word "lot" seventy seven times. I will use several scriptures that pertain to "lot" to give a better understanding and revelation to this term.

Our relationship to the Most High God is predicated on a Covenant. Because of this covenant relationship, every word in the Bible is His promise to us, based upon our obedience to Him. 1st Chronicles 16:18 declares - "To you I will give the land of Canaan." Canaan was a Promised Land for the seed of Abraham. This land (this lot) was established to be possessed for the believer, and only God would bring us to it.

In the Garden

Joshua 17:17-18 states "And Joshua spoke to the house of Joseph-to-Ephraim and Manasseh-saying, "You are a great people and have great power; you shall not have only one lot, but the mountain country shall be yours, and its farthest extent shall be yours; for you shall drive out the Cananites, though they have iron chariots and are strong." This is an awesome promise from God. Here learn that we do not have one singular place set aside for us, but many. God will enable us to drive out the Cananites in our lives, regardless of their strength, because His strength is greater.

Joshua 21:9-10 declares "So they gave from the tribe of the children of Judah and from the tribe of the children of Simeon these cities which are designated by name, which were for the children of Aaron, one of the families of the Kohathties, who were of the children of Levi; for the lot was theirs first." As a co-heir to Christ, our inheritance is intentional, and it has our name on it and no one else's. Our inheritance has been specifically carried down through generations to bless us so that we would be a blessing for the body of Christ. No one can have what God set aside for us.

Psalm 16:5 states, "O Lord, You are the portion of my inheritance and my cup; You maintain my lot." Here the Lord states that the lot we desire is Him and when we come to the full understanding of this, He will give us Himself freely and maintain the Lot He has for us.

Daniel 12:13 is a source of encouragement and direction. "But you go your way til the end; for you shall rest, and will arise to your inheritance at the end of the days." Specific

In the Garden

instruction is implied that we are to press forward till we reach the Lot God set aside for us, wherein we will rest, and then rise up to receive the rewards when we fulfill our purpose. Glory to God in the Highest.

Revelation

When God created me He knew me, and He had already examined me as a lot where He would pour out His Spirit, to do His will, His way. From the beginning He set aside this "Lot" for His Glory. I was part of an apportioned estate. I was to be used as part of an inheritance, as a member of the Body of Christ. He saw me when I was barren waste. He saw me when I had no fruit. But because He knew me, He also knew that I was a lot that could be cultivated and used for His Glory. This lot was connected with the promise that "He who has begun a good work shall perform it until the day of Jesus Christ (Phillipians 1:6). God created this lot—me —to perform a good work wherever He placed me. He set aside lots just for me, which I will receive when I have crossed into the land He has promised through diligence and obedience.

Whether we are examining the lot God has given us to do a work for Him, or whether we are examining ourselves as a lot to be used for God's Glory, consider His word that declares, "He gives all things richly to enjoy." (1st Timothy 6:17)

God's lots are fertile ground, well worth toiling for His Glory.

In the Garden

1. Describe the lot God has given to you at this time. _____

_____

2. Have you found it difficult to accept the lot given to you? _____ Why?

_____

_____

3. Can you describe any current dimensions in your lot that you now realize God is calling you to yield to Him for reorganization? _____

_____

4. In prayer, ask God what is His word to you concerning the lot He has created for you.

_____

_____

5. Are there some lots in your life that are seemingly familiar to you, and you now know that God has been telling you not to return to these places? _____

_____

_____

6. Read 1st Corinthian 1:27. Pray and ask the Lord to reveal the purpose of your lot.

_____

_____

Prayer: Holy and Gracious God My father, thank you for my lot. Help me to acknowledge that you have given this lot to me for "your" Glory. Help me to be humble as I toil this lot. There is much to do in my lot. And I submit myself to you to do the work. You are an awesome God and I count it a privilege to have the blessings that you have set aside for me. To you be all glory, honor and praise. In Jesus Name. Amen

In the Garden

Chapter 2: Prune first

The process of pruning gardens was established for cutting off old unwelcome weeds to enable new growth, to trim, and to cut back for the purpose of producing more growth. Extensive pruning was needed for trees and overgrowth that surrounded the boundaries of my garden. All of the unneeded, dead, and excess plants had to be removed to show the beauty within.

Typically, most plants grown in a garden eventually die or have a flowering cycle that involves death so that life may begin to flourish, similar to the regeneration process. After examining the lot God had given me, I found that parts of it needed to go through a pruning process. This process consisted of examining tree limbs, excess foliage, and death of plant life.

Tree limbs, better known as branches, are an extension of the trunk, and are the basis of the life of a tree. Diseased limbs became hollow and die from the inside out. The true physical health of tree life isn't known until it dies, or isn't conceptualized until dead branches fall off.

The Holy Spirit will lead us through divine insight to thoroughly examine ourselves for things we need to get rid of in our lives. These are the things that are not flourishing, are diseased, unable to produce fruit, or things that we are holding on to that are dead.

In the Garden

Things to prune

There was excess foliage or unnecessary things in my garden. It can come in the form of debris, and disorder. Regardless of how you may identify it or define it, these things could not be used. Think of "these things" as a layer of flesh needing to be pulled off with no comprehensible use, but to weigh you down. Eventually you get tired of the weight that has been placed on you or that you placed upon yourself that is keeping you from performing the tasks God has called you to do.

Purpose of Pruning

God will eventually reveal to you that you can't carry this weight any longer, and that you can't take another step because this excess foliage, debris or ground clutter has had you tripping, stumbling, and falling—holding you in a posture that is disabling you from being a servant He could use. With this revelation, God finally exposes you to things you've carried knowingly or unknowingly that are hindering your growth. These things lead to the destruction of fruit. Can you now see the Holy Spirit revealing to you about the situations that need to be cut down, cut off, or cut away in your life.

Isaiah 18:5 says, "For before the harvest, when the bud is perfect. And the sour grape is ripening in the flower. He will both cut off the sprigs with pruning hooks. And take away and cut down the branches." Here the Lord reveals His purpose for pruning, conditions for pruning to take place, and the tools to be used during the process. Only God could set the stage for this illustriousness brilliance.

Think of it like this: in order for the harvest to come, at the time where what we have sown is ready to give birth, we must be pruned. Before the fruit of our labor bursts forth

In the Garden

pruning is necessary. God will use whatever tools are necessary to remove the remnant from our lives that does not produce fruit. Only God could map out words to describe a process of death and dying, for the purpose of life.

Pruning Tools

Pruning hooks were used to cut away vines to produce a bountiful harvest. The tangled vines linked fruit that grow in abundance on vines. However, not everything that grows on vines produced a good harvest. When gardeners toiling the vineyards found connections to fruit that were of no use, they used pruning hooks and cut the vines and dismantled bad connections. Amen!

Pruning Methods

If you have ever noticed a tree cutter pruning, they methodically cut branches. They targeted branches that have been designated as diseased, dangerous, dead, or those that stunt the growth of other limbs. Pruning trees does not end at limbs being cut off. It also includes the application of a fluid that keeps the limb from being open to infection or bleeding. God in His wonderful way has also included a final process for our pruning. He includes the application of Jesus' blood. When God removes the dead and/or excess, He applies the blood. The pouring in of His Spirit negates the access for the return of dead stuff.

God holds us accountable to bear fruit. John 15:2 states, "Every branch in Me that does not bear fruit He takes away; and every branch that bears fruit He prunes, that it may bear more fruit." The plan of God is revealed here in it's most simplistic manner. If we don't

In the Garden

bring forth what He has placed in us, He will strike us away from Him. As we experience our growth in Christ, God's will takes precedence over everything. He sovereignly prunes us so that life can come forth from death.

The Pruning Process

In Leviticus 25:3, the Lord promises us that for "Six years you shall sow your field, and six years you shall prune your vineyard and gather its fruit " WOW! He has given us specific instructions to sow for an appointed time, go through a pruning process, and then expect a time to gather fruit. Pruning is all part of the process and is not an option. Pruning is necessary for us to bring forth fruit.

The process of pruning in my garden took a substantial amount of time. I pruned from early morning to late afternoon, strategically maneuvering from one end of the garden to the next. I pulled, untangled, followed roots, and cut off limbs. I repeatedly reviewed the garden to make sure I had not left anything that would keep the garden from bringing forth its fruit and showing its true beauty.

Revelation

God in all of His Glory took me through the pruning process where he cut, and dismantled me—down to my deepest roots. He dug deep and exposed my mangled, tattered, torn, and abused spirit. What he left me with was barren to the naked eye. God had left me with fertile ground. I was now willing and seeking to be poured into for His Glory. I did not accept this process immediately, neither will this process ever be complete until He calls me home to Glory, but it was necessary in order for God to make

14

In the Garden

me into who I am becoming for His Glory.

Ecclesiastics 3:1 declares "To everything there is a season, a time for every purpose under heaven." The time for God to prune me came at a point of least expectation. Through His grace, the right pruning was done at the right time, for where God had me planted. Because of His omniscience, omnipotence, and omnipresence, He predestined the exact plan for "this season of pruning." I had to trust God through this process because He promised me in Romans 8:28, "And we know that all things work together for the good to those who love the Lord, to those who are called according to His purpose."

Some symbolize cutting away as a permanent removal. In Christ, death to our flesh is life in Him. The word of God tells us that He came that we may have life and have it more abundantly (John 10:10) and that "We shall not die but live to declare the Glory of the Lord (Psalm 118:17). The release from sin, which is death, gives way to His gifts to us-eternal life. Because of Christ's death we are able to live. Because of my pruning process I can testify that if any man be in Christ he's a new creation, old things are past away, behold He makes all things new (2nd Corinthians 5:17).

I thank God that He would call me to Him, to take me through the pruning process.

Our God is great, and greatly to be Praised.

In the Garden

1. Can you identify area(s) in your life that God is revealing to you that need to be pruned? _____

2. Have these areas needing pruning caused you not to fulfill your purpose in God?
_____

3. As we are often pruned, can you see the timeliness in your last pruning process?
_____

_____

4. Who or what is God using to prune you? _____

_____

5. Pruning includes a methodical approach to applying fluids that keep things that are cut off from infecting others. What area in your life has been pruned that needed the anointing of God to keep from further infecting other areas in your life?
_____

_____

6. Describe God's pruning process in your life. Why do you think He pruned you like this? _____

_____

7. Describe how you felt during the process. _____

_____

8. Describe your final acceptance of God pruning you. _____

_____

Prayer: *God in the precious name of Jesus I come before you praising you for your awesome power. You said that "if any man be in Christ he is a new creation, old things are past away, behold He makes all things new." Thank you Lord for directing the tools for pruning, showing us what needs to be removed from us that you can't use. Even the timing for pruning is perfect. I praise you that you would disengage me from the things that keep me from producing fruit. Lord, I love you and I thank you for your ways are not my ways.*

In the Garden

Chapter3: Weeding

When I began to weed my garden, it was evident that I was way over my head--at times way over my heels, ankles, knees, and arms. It was as though I had come across an abundance of unknown plant life right in my own backyard. I recognized weeds were not the most ideal foliage for my lot, so I opted to remove every weed I could find.

Roots are endless. They lodge themselves beneath the surface, and attach themselves within the dirt. What seemed like a meager task turned into a major production. The more roots I pulled, the more roots I found. I kept saying to myself, "when will I get to the end of the roots?" It was, in fact, just the beginning. I started tearing off the easy weeds around a fence, which were connected to some ground covering near a tree. When it was clearly visible that the surface weeds disappeared, I found myself plucking away at remnant from roots that were embedded in the ground

I stood for many hours bent over, pulling, and tugging at plants that seemed to never end. The more I pulled up roots, the more I could see the roots connected to other roots that were embedded in the lot. So, I kept pulling because I knew that if I didn't continue pursuing the task before me the garden would never become what it was meant to be. There was a point, however, that my natural abilities could not remove all the roots, and overgrowth in the lot. It was then that I applied the strength of an outside source to destroy the roots that seemed to be chasing me.

Definition of weeding

Typically a weed is defined as an unwanted, useless, or troublesome plant that may be injurious to crops and flowers. Gardeners as well as farmers weed to remove these types of plant growth, which routinely choke the life out of productive plants, and leave a path of unwanted foliage. The survival of many flowers and vegetation is contingent on the permanent removal of weeds. Though weeding is conducted in the pruning process, the process of weeding often times includes getting down to deeply embedded roots and using outside sources to destroy them.

Purpose of weeding

The purpose of weeding is to destroy the roots of unwanted plant life. It includes tearing away, uprooting, breaking off, drawing away, lifting up, plucking away, and pulling out. Therein was my task in the Garden. And therein was the spiritual process God was performing in my life.

Contemplation

Have you considered for a moment that something may have lodged itself within you, deep within your surface? Is it pain from a past relationship, fear, unbelief, doubt, oppression, spaces void of peace and joy, hurt from other members of the body of Christ? The list could be endless.

Have you ever considered that you were connected to roots that you believed you were separated from, only to find out that you were still connected to them, after all your efforts to separate yourself from them? Hmm. Though I am speaking of my garden, I am also speaking questions that I had to ask myself.

In the Garden

For a moment, it seemed I was going in a circle, in the garden—not being able to have a permanent break from the roots deep within the ground. I knew the Lord was speaking to me. Roots that were connected to me, that I thought I had been separated from, had to be permanently destroyed. In other words, it was time for me to be weeded out. Is it time for you to be weeded out?

Methods of weeding

There were a variety of methods I could have chosen from, but I have only identified the methods with the best results.

Initially I pulled, and pulled and pulled. Pulling was back breaking, but to those with stamina it's great exercise. That wasn't the case for me. When I pulled I found myself tearing off only parts of the plant. When I took a second glance at what was remaining, I was horrified to find the remaining parts that still needed to be lifted up, uprooted, and plucked away from the depths of my spirit. Oh, I mean my garden!

The weeding process

Because God's word declares in Isaiah 55:8, "For my thoughts are not your thoughts, Nor are your ways My ways," I recognized that He had a different plan for getting to the roots of my weeds. He intended to carefully "not overlook" the roots deeply embedded by the problems "I" had taken on. And He desired to show me how to destroy the many roots that had attached themselves to me, through using His word. To the roots that needed to be torn down He said that I could "cast down every imagination and every high thing that exalts itself against the knowledge of God (2nd Corinthians 10:5). To the roots that

In the Garden

needed to be broken off He told me, " I have broken the bands of yoke and made you walk upright (Leviticus 26:13), and that "He would break in pieces the oppressor" (Psalms72: 4). To the roots that needed to be pulled out He declared to me, " The weapons of our warfare are not carnal but are mighty in God to the pulling down of strongholds" (2nd Corinthians 10:4). To the roots that needed to be drawn away from me, He promised me that His power was greater than anything and that "God draws the mighty away with His power" (Job 24:22). To the roots that needed uprooting He stated "for His kingdom shall be uprooted, even for others besides these" (Daniel 11:4). To the roots that He wanted lifted up He proclaimed, "The Lord makes poor and makes rich; He brings low and lifts up. He raises the poor from the dust, And lifts the beggar from the ash heap, To set them among princes And make them inherit the throne of Glory" (1st Samuel 2:7-8). To the roots that He wanted plucked away He announced, "God shall likewise destroy you forever; He shall take you away, and pluck you out of your dwelling place, And uproot you from the land of the living" (Psalm 52:5). My weeding process included the necessity of an unquestionable belief in Him. And the faith to believe in the ability He had given me, to speak His word over my life.

Are you ready to be weeded? Do you want to use these tools? Or, would you prefer to use some tools more familiar to you? There are a couple of other tools that were not formally used in my garden. However, in my spiritual lot God revealed these additional tools and how to use them.

Have you considered using God's principle of binding and loosing? The word of God in Isaiah 58: 6 tells us that, "Whatever you bind on earth shall be bound in heaven and

In the Garden

whatever you loose on earth shall be loosed in heaven." Through God's spoken word you have to determine in your heart that you can destroy that root within you. And loose the anointing of God to empower you to be liberated from the works and effects of the roots that surround and are embedded in you.

Perhaps there are troubles with your thoughts. "Bring every thought into captivity to the obedience of Christ"(2nd Corinthians 10:5). Our thoughts are to align with Christ! Speak it. Bringing your thoughts into captivity means to have them bound to and connected with Christ. Speak it. Christ is our Intercessor. He is our direct contact with God. We petition to God through Jesus. Jesus goes to the Father and petitions on our behalf. It is through Jesus that God hears, and it is through the Holy Spirit that He moves. Let Him move in your circumstance.

Whatever method you use, remember this: "But you shall receive power when the Holy Spirit has come upon you." (Acts 1:8). And with that power you can speak God's word. As an heir He has given us the power and the authority to speak His word in the name of Jesus. So, now it is done.

Revelation

It was time for me to get it done—to release God to weed out situations from my past, to open my self up to things waiting to be presented to me. It was time to weed out the pain, weed out the tears. It was time to allow God to heal in those deep, dark places. It's not just the top layers God wanted to get to. He had to get to the roots that were often connected to other roots. I could no longer afford to let the weeds choke my life. I could

In the Garden

not allow the weeds to stagnate my growth. God gave me the power of life and death in my tongue. It was time for me to speak life. In Deuteronomy 30:19 God declared that we can chose life so that we and our descendants may live. I choose life. Do you want to be weeded? Have you chosen life?

The word of God in Jeremiah 31:28: declares "And it shall come to pass, that as I have watched over them to pluck up, to break down, to throw down, to destroy, and to afflict, so I will watch over them to build and to plant, says the Lord."

Thank you God for weeding out areas in our lives, and building us back up in your power.

Amen!

In the Garden

1. Can you recognize the weeds in your life? What are they? _____

_____

2. Do you want God to tear away, uproot, break off, draw away, lift up, pluck away, or pull out your weeds. Why? _____

_____

3. Can you trace the origin of your weed(s)? _____

_____

4. Can you recognize the weeds in your life that you tried to detach yourself from that are still lingering in your life? _____

_____

_____

5. Prayerfully seek the Lord and ask Him what process should be used on your weeds.

_____

_____

6. Did you find that in your weeding process you had some weeding responsibilities, God had some weeding responsibilities or that it was a joint effort? _____

_____

Prayer:
Precious Lord, I praise you for showing me the weeds in my life. Though some have been torn away, uprooted, broken off or however you saw fit to remove them, I trust you Lord to make the right decisions for my life. The revelation to the origin of these weeds is but a prayer away. I pray that you in your magnificence would show me their origin so that I can destroy their roots in Jesus' name. Thank you for allowing me to pray to you about my weeds.   Through your strength I went through this process and you most Gracious God did what seemed impossible in the eyes of man. I release you to have your way in my life Lord. In Jesus name I pray.

In the Garden

Chapter 4: Turning over the dirt

The next step in my garden included turning over the dirt. In retrospect, the experience of pruning was nothing compared to turning over dirt. Turning over dirt in my garden was not only dirty, but it was also a hard job. The purpose of turning over dirt was to make the soil ready for planting, or to break up fallow ground.

Definition of fallow ground

Fallow is defined as untilled; uncultivated; neglected; unoccupied; unused; land. All of these terms describe the dirt in my lot. And it was up to me to seek the Lord to bring forth His Glory in the garden.

Process of turning over dirt

I took a systematic approach to turning over the dirt. I started with a shovel—simple enough. Then I determined that the handle was too short to do the job. A neighbor (sent by God) lent me a shovel with a longer handle, which made all the difference in how I approached handling the dirt and turning it over. The longer handle enabled me to dig deeper, to pull up more dirt and turn over more dirt; without additional strain.

When you dig up dirt it's not like when you were a child in a sandlot, placing a shovel everywhere and letting the dirt fly. When my dirt was dug up I used the following process: A hole was dug, the dirt was lifted up and pulled apart from where it was embedded, and then it was turned over to the elements it had not been previously exposed to. Sound, easy enough? But try doing it for hours, digging, lifting, pulling apart, and then turning it over. Performing this task enables you to understand in your own right

In the Garden

that "God's strength is made perfect in weakness." (2nd Corinthians 12:9) Amen!

Digging in my garden entailed performing a transformation. The ground was opened up, dirt was lifted from a lower position to a higher position, and roots were pulled out. The more I worked in the garden to perform these tasks the more I could see God performed a work in me. He selectively opened me up, broke me, and extracted me from my comfort zone by the roots. With His awesome power He turned my whole life around to bring forth a different surface out of me. Nobody but God could do this, or bring forth the depths of this revelation. He brought me to a new level of faith in Him. And He reminded me that," He who has begun a good in you

The Power to get the job done

Just to back up a moment, the shovel is a tool. Its long handle was like the hand of God, which anointed me through the Holy Spirit to do a work for Him. Every dimension to till the ground was not done alone but through the help of God. In everything I did in the garden I recognized "that without Him I could do nothing." (John 15: 5)

Types of dirt

God reminded me about the dirt that I was toiling in the garden. The dirt was issues from the effects of life that seemed insurmountable, and carried a lot of weight. The dry dirt was compacted, whereas the wet dirt easily broken apart. Regardless of the type of dirt it was to be toiled because God had a purpose for its use in my life. Compacted dirt needed more anointing to be broken apart (or to destroy bondage). I observed it to be tightly amassed together. Some of this dirt crumbled immediately when a shovel was applied to it, but some of the dirt was still compacted once the crumbled pieces were removed. When this was the case, more of God's power was needed behind the shovel. The wet dirt, though easily separated, was heavier in consistency. In other words, though the issues of wet dirt could be destroyed quicker, the weight of the effects were more devastating. Though the process for the removal of this dirt was quicker, the strong holds that were applied to my life because of the dirt were deeper.

Consider carrying 100 pounds of dirt on your shoulders indefinitely. There is no relief, only consistent pressure and daily burdens. In Mark 5:25-29, the bible tells us about the woman who lived with the effects of a physical infirmity for years. But the day she reached out to our Savior, He released her from the oppression through His power. Jesus delivered her from her dirt. Do you hear the Savior beckoning you to come to Him to get your dirt removed?

What's in the dirt?

All of my dirt, or all of my issues, had the same ramifications as a result of it being applied to my life. Oppression! I could only be released from the effects of my dirt through God. The dirt was layers of pain, disappointment, abuse, confusion, and misplaced trust in man. It had to be removed so that God could fill me with His joy, peace. And to completely trust in Him.

Though dirt is defined as any foul, or filthy substance, which renders substances unclean or impure, it has its place in our lives in the natural and in the spiritual. Dirt is composed of mud, dirt, excrement, decomposed plant life, and other things seemingly unessential to our lives. Just know that the mud, dirt, excrement, decomposed plant life have a purpose.

In the Garden

Revelation

Without experiencing the foul and filthy places in life, we could never appreciate the promises God made that He is our Hope. Without the dirt and mud thrown on us we could never appreciate God's cultivation of our soil. The dirt enables us to appreciate basking in His presence and Him being a very present help in trouble (Psalms 46:1), and Him promising to hide us under the shadow of His wing (Psalms 17:8)). Without standing in the excrement of our lives, we could never receive the peace that surpasses all understanding (Phillipians 4:7) or joy unspeakable that's full of Glory (1st Peter 1:8). Nor could we comprehend that when we've done all we could to stand, we can stand to see the salvation of the Lord (Exodus 14:13). Without decomposition, we could never see life in death.

Hosea 10:12 - declares "Sow for yourselves righteousness; Reap in mercy; Break up your fallow ground, For it is time to seek the Lord, Till He comes and rains righteousness on you." How fitting it is for the Lord our God to instruct us in purpose for righteousness.

Thank you Lord for showing me the necessity of turning over dirt!

In the Garden

1. What have you observed that God has done to make your soil ready for planting?

_____

_____

2. Define the contents of your dirt and explain your definition. _____

_____

3. Decomposed plant life is often used as fertilizer. Can you see areas in your past that were used as fertilizer? _____

_____

_____

4. Begin to pray and ask God to reveal whether you have dry or wet dirt. _____

_____

5. What's in your dirt that needs to be uncovered? _____

_____

6. Dirt is defined as any foul or filthy substance, which renders substances unclean or impure, and is seemingly unessential to our lives. It does however, have a purpose. Pray and ask God to reveal the purpose of your dirt. _____

_____

_____

Prayer*: Lord God, Maker and Creator of every good and perfect thing I come before you in worship. Praising you for revelation and thanking you for Grace. Lord, you know about the dirt in my life. To the natural eye it has no purpose. So Lord in the name of Jesus open up my eyes to see the spiritual purpose of my dirt. I pray for the anointing to fall upon me to speak against the foul accumulations that have been deposited upon me. Though time has made the wait of deliverance seem forever, thank you for assuring me that You are able to do exceedingly and abundantly above all I could ask or think, but it is according to the power that works within me. It is in the things that seem less worthy of your praise that you divinely purpose for your Glory. Thank you Lord for revealing my dirt.*

In the Garden

Chapter 5: Sowing

Many people feel that they can indiscriminately throw seeds into a garden, and a bountiful array of beautiful flowers will spring forth. The variety of seeds in nature is innumerable. It may produce rich colors or tropical green. Some plants may be low-ground covering plants or plants of extreme heights. There are some seeds that produce a natural ability to heal and others that can make you sick or even kill you. Regardless of the distinguishing characteristics in seeds, it is impossible to know the origin of every seed, or the effects of sowing a multitude of seeds together. Whenever and wherever seeds are sown, we have to be careful that the seeds sown are beneficial, not detrimental.

The sowing process

The course of nature or the natural process for seeds to spring forth takes place whether the seed is placed in a hole in the ground or scattered randomly. But God, who directs nature, takes over and initiates the process for seeds to be planted and mature. God divinely takes a seed to be placed where it can be rooted in a dormant spot of dirt, seemingly uncultivated and unfertilized, to spring forth for His god pleasure. This progression is similar to when God called His people. He took us, planted us in places of uncertainty, where we seemed unproductive, and at times where we gave the appearance that we were alone, But He promised "Lo I am with you always," (Matthew 28:20) wherever he plants us!

The order of sowing

The natural order of sowing takes place in the fall before the first frost, or in the early spring. Bulbs are planted during the fall and seeds are sown in early spring. Seeds and bulbs have a synchronized clock for when they take root, become fertilized within the ground, and open up. It is automatic for them. No bulb that should be planted in the fall comes forth in the spring, if it is planted in dead winter. It doesn't produce anything. It's just dead.

We, too, are sown into the earth for a particular order of flowering. Jeremiah 29:11 tells us that "I know the plans I have for you declares the Lord, plans to prosper not to harm, for a future and a hope." God is a predestinator. He predestined us before we were in our mother's womb, and before we were born He sanctified us for His Glory." This is the God that we serve. It is not a fluke of nature that we are here. Nothing that occurs in our life happened without His knowledge. Everything that ever took place was part of the equation He set in place for us. God's word tells us "For who He foreknew, He also predestined to be conformed to the image of His Son, that He might be the firstborn among many brethren. Moreover who He predestined, these He also called; who He called, these He also justified, and who He justified, and these He also glorified." (Romans 8:29-30). God sowed His purpose when He breathed life into us.

Just as God has sown seeds abundantly into His people for His purpose, we too have a multitude of seeds within us available to be sown into others. Some are good and some are not. It is through our perfecting process that our "bad seeds" are cut off, cut back, and destroyed. As we know that there is none perfect but our Lord and Savior Jesus Christ, we also recognize that as a co-heir in the kingdom of God we are created in His image. Life's experiences often take us off our perfecting track. But the good news is that God still seeks to perfect us to mirror his image. His perfection process involves taking away those things within us that are not like him including our attitudes and behaviors. It is extremely necessary to safeguard against administering corruptible seeds

What seeds are you sowing?

Be aware of the seeds you are sowing. God holds us accountable for what we sow into other people. Sowing involves conveying information into another person. Seeds are often relayed through our mouth. The word of God tells us that "death and life are in the power of the tongue." (Proverbs 18:21) Therefore, we must be careful what we say to one another. Through God's spoken word we have the ability to create an atmosphere when we speak. It is through our thoughts and mind that our atmosphere is developed. If we have had negative impartations, we will formulate a negative atmosphere.

Our Heavenly Father, however, gives us a counter attack for this. He says, "For the weapons of our warfare are not carnal, but are mighty in God to the pulling down strong holds." (2nd Corinthians 10:4) In defense of the non-fruit producing seeds that have been spoken to us and around us, we have God's word to destroy the works of Satan.

Other means of sowing seeds come in the form of the gifts, talents, and abilities which have been given to us by God for His people. In Ephesians 4:11-13, it says, "and He Himself gave some to be apostles, some prophets, some evangelists, and some pastors and teachers, for the equipping of the saints for the work of ministry, for the edifying of the body of Christ, till we all come to the unity of the faith and of the knowledge of the

In the Garden

Son of God, to perfect man, to the measure of the stature of the fullness of Christ." The seeds within us have been designated for a purpose and "the gifts and callings of God are without repentance."(Romans 11:29)

They cannot be ignored and are not to be received in sorrow. It is up to us to seek the Lord, find out what path He has called us for, and in what capacity within that calling we are to serve Him with our seeds. "He" has placed in us every gift, talent, and ability. Remember the parables about the talents in Matthew 25:15-29. Talents have been placed within us to carry along our journey to bear fruit, not to be left in the ground to be hidden. We don't want to be recognized as an unprofitable servant. Understand that this is a building process even in sowing, as we are faithful over a few things, He will make us rulers over many."(Matthew 25:23) God is mindful to tell us in Zechariah 10:9, " I will sow them among the peoples." Therefore we do have purpose, for His Glory.

The ground where you sow

The parables of Jesus in Matthew 13: 1-7 talks of the sower whose deposits were devoured, withered away because they had no root, fell among thorns and were choked, and those deposits that fell on good ground and yielded a crop some of a hundred fold. God often reminds us to be knowledgeable of where and to whom we sow. Your seed cannot be planted just anywhere with anyone. As God is a God of order, there is an assignment for your deposit.   It is to be deposited in a place to build God's Kingdom. Your tests, your trials, have all been purposed, so that God's Glory will show through in the victory. And that you will be able to deposit into another, God's ministering power to

In the Garden

defeat the enemy, to set captivity captive, to destroy yokes, and to lift burdens. You are a designated hitter for God. The seed implanted in you is for the deliverance of another.

Where we sow is just as important as to whom we sow into. Jeremiah 4:3 reminds us not to sow among thorns. Thorns are prickly places that are raised up to cause pain, that pierce, oppress, and are destructive. If our seeds have a designated assignment, we should not initiate sowing into places that would serve to be destructive or oppressive, to that which God has set aside to guide spiritually. God's word declares, "do not cast your pearls before swine, lest they trample them under their feet, and turn and tear you in pieces (Matthew 7:6) In Leviticus 26:16 we are encouraged to "Not to sow in vain, for your enemies shall eat it." Our enemies eating that which is to be sown, confirms that sowing in the wrong places will lead to the devouring of seed that has been placed in us for purpose.

Why sow?

At one point I thought, "why continue the process of sowing seeds in my garden." Surely, to get a harvest! But the worked seemed too difficult, just trying to figure out what was to go where. In my mind I began to try to reason and justify the outlay of intense labor from me, to reap a garden that only God could arrange. Through the revelation from Phillipians 1:6 "He who has begun a good work in you, shall perform it unto the day of Jesus Christ", it was clear to me that I didn't sow anything in my garden. I didn't do any of the work. God did all the work, through me. His purpose for sowing seeds into me was to do a work through me, for His harvest. It is our purpose according to God's word in

In the Garden

Matthew 13:38, to" be sown as good seeds throughout the fields of the earth", and accordingly in Matthew 13:30, "so that His harvest be gathered into His barns."

Revelation

There was a major revelation received through sowing seeds in my garden. God showed me that it was not by chance that I was sown into the world at this time, and that there is a specific order even to sowing. Isaiah 32:20 declares "Blessed are those that sow beside all waters." As this refers to the seeds of the gospel, to whomever "He" sends me to sow, I must sow regardless of their place in the Kingdom. His words of wisdom reveal the mysteries of sowing and reaping in 2nd Corinthians 9:6 to "sow bountifully to reap bountifully." Galatians 6:8 warns us to" sow to the Spirit to reap everlasting life." Amen.

Psalms 126:5-6 says, "Those who sow in tears shall reap in joy." I sowed why tears for many years because "I" did not fully know what God was going to do with me, especially during difficult situations. But one day I did understand. And I stopped sowing why tears and began sowing His word into my life. His word is His promise to me because of our covenant relationship. When I began to acknowledge this great revelation I began to reap joy. I believed Him. I trusted Him. I knew that He was my strong tower. I now sow tears of "gladness" for who God is to me. He is God. He is my God. He is the lover of my soul.

At the beginning of my Christian walk I never knew the depths of the relationship that I would have with the Lord. The more I study His word and pray, the more He unlocks the mysteries of His Kingdom. Being sown in His garden is yet another way for Him to

In the Garden

reveal Himself and my purpose for Him. Just think, even in His word He tells us that "For indeed I am for you, and I will turn to you, and you shall be tilled and sown (Ezekiel 36:9)

Praise be to our Mighty God, "for the sower sows the word'" (Mark 4:14)

In the Garden

1. Prayerfully seek the Lord and ask Him to reveal to you about the seeds you've sown.

_____

_____

2. Write down the place(s) of uncertainty God has sown you and then wondrously revealed to you that this is His good pleasure. _____

_____

3. Do you recognize God's synchronized clock for when your seeds rooted, became fertilized, and bloomed? _____

_____

4. Have the seeds you've sown helped to build up or tear down people.

_____

_____

5. Ask God to show you how and where to use your counter attack tools in 2nd Corinthians 10:4. _____

_____

6. Do you know the purpose of the seed God has placed within you? _____

_____

Prayer: *Father God, your word has been a light unto my feet and a lamp unto my path. It is to you that I honor with the lips of my praise. I magnify you because you are the Holy God of Israel. Father, allow the Holy Spirit to resonate within me daily. Remind me that you have purposely sown into me many seeds to sow throughout the nations where you send me. Please God, continue to purify me so that these seeds I sow are worthy of your Glory. Help me to see that there is divine order to even sowing, and that you are doing all of the work in my garden.*

In the Garden

Chapter 6: Watering

Water! The substance of life! It is through water that we are refreshed, renewed, revived, replenished, repaired, and restored. Nothing can live without it. The year I planted my garden there was a drought. God, in His infinite power, ordained rain upon my garden at specifically directed intervals, to bring forth His glory, in my garden.

After cultivating, pruning, and sowing seeds, I knew that there would be no growth without water. Though my garden was small, water was a needed element. Watering was necessary for the seeds to open, root, and begin flowering. I began my planting process in late spring, but by the time I had finished, it was early summer. It was now hot, dry, and humid, and it was not the best climate for plant growth.

I knew that if I went this far in the gardening process I had to remain faithful until the plant matured. I didn't water the plants often because I saw clouds rolling in, and assumed it was going to rain. It didn't. This happened repeatedly over the course of many weeks and needless to say my flowers were not in the best condition. I had to stop looking at what I perceived to be rain rolling in on clouds, and water the flowers regardless of what I perceived. The plants looked bad, justifiably. Therefore I had to honestly make a concerted effort to water my plants. If the plants were not watered they would die.

Do you see God in this picture? He is the water that we need. We can't live without him, and He reigns upon us at designated intervals of our maturity process, for His glory. As

In the Garden

indicated in Psalm 72:6 "He shall come down like rain upon the grass before mowing, Like showers that water the earth." God, the Gardener, recognizes that "we" need lots of water in order to become what He has called us to be. And though the climate of our growth is not always optimal for us, from where we stand, He remains faithful until we reach the fullness of Christ. God has given us each an assignment to pour into the body of Christ through our assigned gifts. He makes a vow to us in Proverbs 11:25 that states, "And he who waters will also be watered himself." Not to say that this is the only way in which He reveals himself. He always uses His spirit, which reveals all truths to teach us that He is life.

The Purpose of water

Water in its most natural state is used to wash, drink, cleanse, purify, and irrigate plant life. Only under the power of the Holy Spirit is it used to:

- Quench the supernatural thirst for the word of God, "Ho! Everyone who thirst, Come to the waters (Isaiah 55:1);
- Heal, "In these lay a great multitude of sick people, blind, lame, paralyzed, waiting for the moving of the water" (John 5:3);
- Cleanse the sin sick soul," that He might sanctify and cleanse her with the washing of water by the word," (Ephesians 5:26).

Usage and forms of water

The life of a garden is contingent on its source and adequate use of water. Similarly, the body of Christ also requires water. The Old and New Testament speaks of many forms of water that was used to bring forth a message from God to His people. God used Noah to warn the people of retribution through floodwaters as a result of their disobedience. God used the parting of the Jordan River to show a path of deliverance for His people being

In the Garden

delivered from the hands of Pharaoh. God also used water to heal at the pool of Bethesda.

Where is God in the water?

God revealed His character to me in the water. He showed me that He is the fountain of living waters according to Jeremiah 2:13, and 17:13. Through His watering I became alive. In the water He showed me that He is my spiritual provision and replenisher. This is indicated in Isaiah 44:3 "For I will pour water on Him who is thirsty, and floods on the dry ground, therefore meeting my every need. Even in the uncultivated, uninhabited places God has sent me, He constantly thinks of me, and has left His spirit to comfort me as indicated in Isaiah 43:20, "Because I give waters in the wilderness And rivers in the desert."

What's in the water?

In the water God reveals Himself, the promise of hope in Him, His wonders, and His spirit. He performs a metamorphosis unduplicated by man's own ability.

Revelation

My garden relied upon water as the substance of life. It was up to me to saturate the garden with the natural life sustaining substance, for it to flourish and survive. I thank God that I can rely upon Him more than my garden could rely upon me, to saturate me with His water. God never forgets to pour out His spirit upon me. God's plan wasn't to wait on something or someone else to do a job to bring me to fulfillment. He did it Himself. Thought I was barren God nurtured me to be who He has called me to be. He gave me the exact amounts of His life sustaining substance at the right time. He didn't

In the Garden

leave me alone to wonder if He was going to fulfill the promises that He had made for me. He didn't leave me for dead.

Water promotes growth. Plant life needs water, and our physical body needs constant replenishing. Even so, the people of God need to replenish our water supply often, through Him. The scriptures in Ezekiel 31:4 reveals God's mighty power, "The waters made it grow; Underground waters gave it height, With their rivers running around the place where it was planted, And sent out rivulets to all the trees of the field." Take a moment now and go before Him. Let Him saturate you with His spirit to make you grow. The word of God in Job 14:9 declares that, "Yet at the scent of water it will bud, And bring forth branches like a plant."

Blessed be the name of the Lord!

In the Garden

1. How is God using water to refresh, revive, or restore your life? _____

_____

2. Read Proverbs 11:25. Begin to pray. What are you thirsting for from God? _____

_____

_____

3. How much of God's water do you want and why? _____

_____

_____

4. What is the purpose of God watering you? _____

_____

_____

5. God used water to relay a message to His people often throughout the Bible. What message is God speaking to you through watering you? _____

_____

_____

6. Read Job 14:9. Now begin to pray. Ask God "Am I solely relying upon you to give me your life sustaining water"? _____

_____

_____

Prayer: Lord of my life, I lift up your name because you are the only true and living God. You continue to show me that there is no other worthy of the praise but you. The life in your water has refreshed, restored, renewed, revived, and repaired me. Thank you for allowing your water to fall afresh upon me. You Most High God have ordained my watering. Please God allow your water to fill me. Now that your spirit has come upon me I have received your power. Thank you for allowing your spirit of truth and the comforter to be with me. Every droplet of water has purpose and for this I give you praise.

In the Garden

Chapter 7: Blooming

One by one the petals opened and the flowers bloomed in my garden. There were deep vibrant colors and mixtures of plants creating a picture of natural harmony. The petunias, assorted lilies, wild flowers, dandelions, and hostas immediately draw the eye as you look upon the "garden". The garden had come alive.

God Blooms Sovereignly

Life in the garden didn't start at the time where I could see the flowers bloom. It started at the point where seeds and bulbs were initially planted. It was there that God was performing a miracle. The miracle came through the works of His hands that took each seed, deposited it into fertile soil, allowed it to root downward, so that the flower could spring forth upward. God does things so differently than us. He takes you down to the depths of life, to come forth with His power, as indicated in 2nd Kings 19:30 "And the remnant who have escaped of the house of Judah shall again take root downward, and bear fruit upward."

When a seed matures into a flower it develops into three distinct parts. The first part of the flower is the petals, symbolic of God's loving arms that embrace us. Next is the stem, a focal point to demonstrate God's strength. This is the evidence of His powerful hand that holds us. And lastly, the roots of the flower represent the depth of the indwelling of the Holy Spirit within us, that guide us and reveals all truths. At the point where the flower completely blooms, there is another metamorphosis. The flowers' petals raise up to worship the Lord. The stem of the flower becomes elongated and strong, not wavering in storms. And the roots of the flower are planted firmly. It is in the garden, where we are" fearfully and wonderfully made, marvelous are thy works." (Psalms 139:14)

In the Garden

Lovingly, God's fingers massage each flower and allow it to blossom at just the right time of maturity. Gently, and purposefully every predestined petal is pulled open to reveal, (though some might think a flower) it is, His Glory. Inside each petal lies life. The life that He promised is in His Son Jesus Christ, the Anointed One.

Life in the garden

Life in the garden is evident by the production of fruit and is defined as "offspring" or "result of an action". The word of God in Matthew 12:33 declares, "for a tree is known by its fruit. In the garden God revealed the fruit of purpose, confidence, discipline, God-dependency, waiting, love, and the power in the name of Jesus."

Fruit of Purpose

In the garden, I accepted my purpose and the importance of the gifts that God had given me for His kingdom. I stopped running from what I was created for. I did not deny that I was first created to love Him, but I was also created to do a work for Him that no one else was created to do. I accepted my job, my purpose, knowing that I couldn't do it without Him because, "His strength is made perfect in my weakness (2nd Corinthians 12:9)

Fruit of Confidence

Ah, the fruit of confidence. In the garden confidence was unleashed. This fruit took its time and grew slowly. The moment this fruit began to sprout, it acted as a catalyst, shooting up more flowers around itself until it was inundated with it's own fruit. It constantly regenerated itself. The spirit of doubt was cast down, and the spirit of certainty was unveiled. Confidence in my Lord and Savior Jesus Christ flourished.

In the Garden

Instead of just having the knowledge to say, "This is the confidence that I have in approaching God "(John 14:15), God birthed inside of me the connection in the spirit to speak these words into existence over every prayer, knowing that I really believed in Him and that He was finally real to me.

Fruit of Discipline

Though there is no discipline for how flowers grow in the garden, God taught me the benefits of being disciplined. Unlike some flowers that grow totally out of control, God has complete control over how we grow—in His image after His own likeness (Genesis 1:27) Being undisciplined to God's development process comes at a high price. I do not recommend it. Disciplined does not mean that you take on a repetitive nature to accomplish a goal. It means that there is an inherent desire to accomplish, conduct or complete a task where the benefits outweigh the output of labor, no matter what that labor may be. I became disciplined to study His word because I was thirsty. I became disciplined to pray because I desired communication with the Most High God. I became disciplined to seek opportunities for Praise and Worship because I wanted to thank God for His mercies and bless Him for His faithfulness to me. I became disciplined to acknowledge and speak in the name of Jesus Christ because He is my Savior. Through the fruit of discipline God showed me that He could trust me and "show me great and unsearchable things I did not know." (Jeremiah 33:3)

Fruit of God-dependency

I was used to being self-reliant, not God dependent. Lessons learned from releasing my dependency unto the Lord far outweighed my own abilities. He gave me His word that "I

In the Garden

could cast all of my cares upon Him for He cares for me." (1st Peter 5:7)   God dependency assured me I had no need to worry, but to "Be anxious for nothing, but by prayer, supplication, with thanksgiving, make my request known unto the Lord (Phillipians 4:6)." Never again will I need to worry. I could never tell you that this part of my process went smoothly. It didn't. God was building up faith, through my dependency on Him. I was challenged to believe in the unbelievable, and to do the inconceivable. I was put in a position that if God didn't do it; it wasn't going to get done. No friends, no family, nothing and no one else could I rely upon - accept for God. One of the most powerful lessons I learned in submitting to God dependency was that I was submitting myself for God's plan, knowing that if I entrusted God to answer my prayer, the answer to the prayer would always be far greater than what I could do for myself.

Fruit of Waiting

One of my favorite scriptures comes from Isaiah 40:31, "They that wait upon the Lord shall renew their strength, they shall mount up on wings like eagles. They shall run and not get weary. They shall walk and not faint." God taught me the meaning of waiting while in the Garden. Though waiting it is not just a stationary posture, it is however, a position of servitude towards the Lord. I received the revelation through waiting on God that He had already worked out my situations and fulfilled His promises to me. I could not just sit idly and expect a transformation in my life. I had to do "something." That something was serving the Lord with the gifts He had given me, which included humble service that I might never be recognized for, but in my heart I knew that it pleased the Lord. I sowed into people's lives with the anointing God had given me. Time and time

In the Garden

again I found confirmation that I was doing His will because I experienced that "His burden is easy and His yoke is light,"(Matthew 11:30). Doing what He called me to do, and not what He called another to do, did not over task me. It was however, up to me, to seek the Lord to find out what He wanted me to do, for Him. And that too came through" waiting on the Lord and being of good courage"(Psalms 27:14). My waiting process developed an increased level of endurance that lent increased strength to the dressings of my armor.

Fruit of God's Love

John 3:16 says, "For God so loved the world that He gave His only begotten son, that whosoever believeth in Him shall not parish but have everlasting life." Birthing the fruit of love could only be done through God. God's love is unconditional, open, unreserved, unrestricted, free, and forgiving. Though love can be defined further, I had to be taught and experience these aspects of God's love. His love is what best describes His attitude towards His people, shown through His actions, through the gifts He gives us. As followers of Christ we are to show our love towards Him, demonstrated through our obedience. And equally so, our love is demonstrated by the way we treat others. We were created to be a benefit towards the welfare of others.

Before I developed a relationship with God, I could only associate love as a physical means of expression. The type of love that is conveyed through being exposed to His son - is spiritual. It produces a transfiguration. Exposure to love through the Son means I no longer have to look towards man to love me as a feeling of comfort. I am now comforted daily by the loving arms of God. Because He loves me, He is my protection and provision. His love is consistent and dependable. The love of God allowed Jesus to die

46

In the Garden

for my sin though he never committed sin.

Fruit of acknowledging the power in the name of Jesus

Jesus, the name above every name. The scriptures tell us that, "At the name of Jesus every knee shall bow and every tongue confess that Jesus is Lord" (Phillipians 2:10). He is my Savior, my Lord. I am a witness to the power in His name! He is the one who chose the nails for me, was ransomed for my soul, whose existence was to die that I might be free. Because of this I am able to call Him:

> Counselor. Lamb of God. King of Kings. Lord of Lords. Faithful and True Witness. Rock. Living Water. Bread of Life. True Vine. Teacher. Prophet. Mediator. Carpenter. Servant. Bridegroom. Only begotten Son. The Way, the Truth, and the Life. Redeemer!

The scriptures tell us that on the third day Jesus got up out of the grave, and rose up with all power in His hands. I met Jesus in my garden. And He showed me, His power.

Looking back at the original lot, there was no evidence that something of this magnitude could ever come to being, but God outstretched His mighty hand and transformed "this lot" for His magnificence. The garden was saved from being a place of destitute overgrowth, idly stationed, with no purpose. The garden was revived to bring forth life. The garden was restored because God promised in His word that, "He restoreth my soul." (Psalm 23:3) And the garden was created so that the flowers would live! The word of God declares that "I shall not die but live, and declare the Glory of the Lord" (Psalms 118:17). Life was saturated throughout the Garden! It had come into a state of existence.

Thank you God for life in the Garden. I love you Lord.

In the Garden

1. Have your petals opened to reveal the life that God has created in you? _____

_____

_____

2. Read 2nd Kings 19:30. Pray and ask God to reveal to you what has taken root and what has bore fruit. _____

_____

3. Can you see yourself as God's flower, with petals that are comforted by God's loving arms, with a stem held up by God's strong arms, and with roots directed by the indwelling of the Holy Spirit? What has each part of the flower personally symbolized to you?

_____

_____

4. Read Matthew 12:33. What are you known by? Pray and ask God to reveal your fruits. _____

_____

5. Have you recognized that you have bloomed through the anointing of Jesus for God?

_____

_____

6. Look back at God's regenerating power and describe what God has done, so that you could bloom. _____

_____

Prayer: *Father, I love you and I adore you. I bless you for being faithful. It is because of you that there is life in the Garden. Help me to remember that your timing is perfect, and to everything there is a season. You father, have lifted the chains of oppression and have saturated me with your love. And because of your love there is fruit in the garden. Blessed be the name of the Lord.*

In the Garden

Chapter 8: Rising to meet the Son in the Garden

One late afternoon, in early summer, while gazing at my Garden, I noticed a Lilly. The more I looked at this Lilly, I couldn't help but focus on the posture of the Lilly, the vibrant colors of its flowering head, and the unusually long green stem. The flower seemed to be leaning at an angle as if it were trying to catch the rays of the sun. It was here that I saw God in all His Glory. The sun in the sky was not actually what I saw. The flower in the garden was not a Lilly. The flower in the garden was me, and the sun in the sky was the Son of God.

I arose to find the Son whose unconditional love is inconceivable. Basking in His presence, He showed me that it was okay to lean towards Him and that He is and will always be my Savior. I was leaning because He was calling. He was beckoning me to rest in Him. My Father which art in Heaven had pursued me. He told me He had something special just for me--gifts. I wanted the gifts of His presence, His Son, His word, His anointing.

Exposed to the Son

The special, made to order gifts that God had prepared for me came at a price. The price I paid for His gifts was giving up everything that I was used to being and having. Many times I could not understand what was happening to me, that is, before I came to know the Lord Jesus Christ, through a personal relationship. Now I have peace, as I recognized that there were things within me that God could not use. I found myself being stripped of almost everything, including my mind. Things and people were taken away, situations

49

In the Garden

arose that were completely out of my control. Why? Because God wanted to show off His Glory. He wanted to show me that He would do everything and be everything for me. Empowering me for His purpose was His goal. The attitudes and behaviors in my life would not give Him Glory. And God had to expose these strongholds to the light of His Son, to be destroyed, so that I could be free.

My strongholds included the spirit of self-centeredness, self-sufficiency, impatience, lost confidence, the inability to trust God that I could move in His power, and the inability to speak out against the demonic attacks that sought to destroy me and my family. I am honestly speaking these truths of revelation in the hopes that if there are others in the same situation, that they would recognize these yokes of bondage, and seek the strength of God's power to fight against these and other spirits.

God sought to deliver me from things deep within. I was taken out of the world that "I" had created for me, to a world totally centered on God. A transfiguration took place, to change my life to solely revolving around God. I now sought the things of God, the Lord's direction, and His wisdom for everything going on in my life.

I was self-centered. The character of my self centeredness included my "self" confidence, my "self" affirmation, viewing situations from a human perspective, and dependence on my own abilities. Praise be to God that He wanted me to be God-centered which is confidence in God, being humble before him, seeking God's perspective through my circumstances, and total dependence on His ability for provision.

The transfiguration of self-centeredness to God-centeredness led me to painful trials, as well as a multitude of blessings. In addition, the gifts God had placed within me began to manifest. I was now becoming His woman. And he had kept me through this process.

I marveled at the destruction of the self-sufficiency stronghold. The pain of separation from this stronghold came from years of "I don't need anybody's help" and "I can and will do it myself." I was miss independent and able to handle anything that came my way. God's plan was for Him to do everything and be everything to me. He placed me in numerous seasons (until I finally got the point) where He took "my" ability away from me. And lead me to the path of His ability. That was done through prayer, reading His word, His Son, and the Holy Spirit. He introduced me to Jehova El-Shaddai. The Lord God Almighty.

I am glad now that I now know God to be my everything. I no longer have to depend on man for anything. God gave me His word, which was His promise through our covenant relationship. And all I had to do was trust and believe that He is. He said in His word that He is able to do exceeding and abundantly above all I could ask or think, according to the power that works within me (Ephesians 3:20). He told me "Now this is the confidence that we have in approaching Him, that if we pray according to His will, He hears us. And if we know that He hears us, whatever we ask, we know that we have the petitions that we have asked of Him." (1st John 5:14); He told me that'" no good thing will He withhold from them that walk uprightly (Psalms 84:11); He told me in His word "I have never seen the righteous forsaken, Nor His seed begging bread. (Psalms 37: 25)

Increased faith
I found myself without transportation for many months because my car had a broken head gasket and I had no money to get it fixed. I was paying a car note without being able to

In the Garden

drive the car. The car was outside of the warranty period, and I didn't believe that I would be able to get the car fixed, but God was building up my faith in Him. He was loosing me from my own selfish pride and ability. So the car sat, and sat. And one day while discussing the car situation with a brother from the church, He encouraged me to write a letter to the car manufacturer. Keep in mind that I had been praying "God direct me to the path I am to take for this situation." After contemplating writing the letter, for too long, (the slothful/procrastination-spirit), I finally sent a letter to the manufacturer, who never officially answered my letter. I called them exactly 26 days after sending my letter. That Tuesday afternoon, I was informed that they received the letter within four days of my mailing, but that the letter was at the bottom of a huge pile. I was instructed to get the car to the dealership the best way I could (without their towing assistance), and be prepared to pay a diagnostic fee (did I tell you I wasn't working at the time). I stepped out on faith and slowly drove the car to the dealership that Friday, believing that God would provide. At the end of the day I received a phone call with good news and bad news. The bad news was that they confirmed the car had a blown head gasket, which would cost a total of $800 instead of the original $1200.00 that was quoted to me. The seemingly good news was that the manufacturer would provide a one-time good will offer to me and allow me to pay only $400.00 (I believe I told you previously that I wasn't working). I inquired as to who had made the decision, and the service man refused to give me that information. I told him I would call back on Monday to inform him of my decision to get the car fixed. This gave me an entire weekend to pray. That Monday afternoon I called back to the manufacturer, through the leading of the Holy Spirit and once again received the favor of God. I informed them of my financial hardship and the representative

In the Garden

informed me that they would once again refer me for special consideration. I continued to pray and seek the Lord. Within 2 days I received a phone call from the dealership, from a different service man, wherein the conversation started like this. "For some reason-and I don't know why, for all the work that you need done to your car, the price of this huge job will only be $100.00." Well I was excited but I had so much more to give God the Glory for. I was also told that I needed the cooling system flushed, a thermostat, and a tune-up. I again asked the dealership if they were willing to make a payment arrangement on these additional items totaling over $300.00.

And that's when the service man put me on hold. Do you know what can be done when you put a Christian on hold? Did I pray! Through the 2-3 minutes I was put on hold I gave God the Praise for what He had done and for what He was about to do. When the service man came back to the phone he stated that he was unable to get in touch with a manger, but would see what he could do to at least get the system flushed. Miracles did not cease that afternoon. I came home to $40.00 in cash in an envelope as well as an unexpected $25.00 check, to put towards my $100.00 charge for getting $1200.00 worth of work conducted. Glory.

Throughout all of this I kept giving God the Glory and Praise, and seeking him to fulfill his promises to me that "my God shall supply all your needs according to His riches in Glory by Christ Jesus." (Phillipians 4:19). It was because I no longer moved in my own strength but sought His strength and His performance of miracles in my life.

I came to the full knowledge that there is no other God in the universe. He had control over every one of my situations because He said in His word "For I know the plans I have for you declares the Lord, plans to prosper and not to harm, for a future and a hope (Jeremiah 29:11).

Impatience was another attribute that could not be used in the vineyard of God's people. The stronghold of impatience by definition refers to one's inability to wait, irritation at having to wait, and intolerant. I no longer want to be defined by this word. There is no way I could have honored God carrying this spirit. This ongoing fight was a battle of the spirit fighting against the flesh. "For the flesh lusteth against the spirit, and the Spirit against the flesh; and these are contrary the one to the other; so that ye cannot do the things that ye would, is referred to in (Galatians 5:17).

This could be better described as an endless rope-pulling contest. Back and forth the contestants pulled. Here you have the Holy Spirit trying to purge man from a layer of flesh that has resided upon us, for no Godly purpose. A form of physical exertion finally culminated. And it was at this point that it wasn't about one's individual strength, but that the winner's strength is determined by the belief in the power of the Almighty God for deliverance. The word of God tells us in Romans 4:20 that we are to," be fully persuaded that God has the power to do what He had promised." God had the power to remove this unwanted and unneeded layer of flesh, because I knew from previous experience that it was not bearing fruit.

Another early summer morning while walking with my son, I began to meditate over the definition of impatient and the word intolerant jumped out of my spirit. God was telling me that instead of being tolerant of the things that were happening and the situations that I was being positioned into by His mighty hands, that I was being intolerant. "I" never perceived myself as intolerant, but God showed me that "I" was. And I am sure you don't see yourself as being intolerant, do you?

He began to show me that if He was intolerant of everything that happened since creation, that He would never have given us His Son Jesus, the blood, or Salvation. And so I began to yield my intolerance to Him and my patience increased. I began to seek to be swift to hear, slow to speak, slow to wrath (James 1:19). A sweeter, kinder, spirit within me had begun to develop. My flesh was subject to the spirit of Christ. The major revelation from being In the Garden was that the more I pursued the Son of God, the less I had use of my flesh, and the more I sought the Spirit.

I thank God for being all seeing, all knowing, everywhere. What a wonderful God! Rather that punish me, He gave me a venue to come to Him, repent, ask for forgiveness, yield the "stuff" that He's showed me He can't use, and mold this vessel for His Glory.

Rising towards the Son made me face my own inability to totally trust in the anointing of God. I had received the Holy Spirit. The anointing was working throughout my life. Why couldn't I totally trust? Why couldn't I fully believe in the anointing and that the full power of the anointed one was real. The anointing of God was real. My anointing was real. What more did I need? The Holy One had touched me. I was allowed to be ushered into the presence of the Almighty, to touch the hem of His garment. I was allowed to speak and pray in the name of the anointed one. To be given the ability to utter promises

In the Garden

in the name of my Lord and Savior Jesus Christ should have been enough.

I was taught that the anointing was the power we receive through the Holy Ghost, from the Son of God. What was it that kept me from moving fully in Him? Why couldn't I fully believe in the anointing? Simply, I had to believe from the depths of my spirit that He was, is, and shall always be. I had to understand fully that "He that cometh to God must believe that He is, and that He is ", (Hebrews 11: 6).

Walking with the Son

Some might say that yielding my trust in the anointing of God should have been easy. At first it was not. I had knowledge of the anointing, through many teachings. I had acknowledged the anointing to be real, evident through seeing its power working through the lives of others. But for me to actually be walking in the anointing, for me to have the power, I just didn't see myself as a co-heir to Christ. The personal belief of the anointing came through the diligent reading of God's word and through prayer. Only God could instill the belief of Him and His power, in me. I had to trust God to know that the same spirit that dwelled in Christ Jesus, also dwelled in me. I had to believe that walking the path of a disciple of Jesus Christ gave me the abilities to perform works for the Father who is in Heaven.

Walking in the power of the anointing you experience movement in the spiritual realm. You experience God! God endows you with a spiritual eye, different from how you see things in the natural. You come to a place in God where you recognize that before you were in your mother's womb he knew you (Jeremiah 1:5), and that God had placed

In the Garden

specific gifts, talents, and abilities within you to serve His kingdom. In Ephesians 4:11-12 we are reminded that, "And He himself gave some to be apostles, some prophets, some evangelists, and some pastors and teachers, for the equipping of the saints for the work of ministry, for the edifying of the body of Christ." Walking in the power of the anointing you recognize that "It is He who made us, and not we ourselves." (Psalms 100:3). You recognize that you are a child of the King, co-heir to our Savior Jesus Christ that you are from the seed of Abraham, that Salvation is free, and that you were bought with a price. Walking in the anointing of God, I see through God's ability, that I trust in the anointing of God, and that I submit my life to prayer, worship, and praising the Lord Most High.

Using words spoken by the Son

Rising towards the Son of God also meant that I had the power to pray against the works of the Devil. So why had I been in bondage for years? Why didn't I just speak against every situation that "I" allowed to torment me? Why hadn't I spoken against the pits and pitfalls that came against me? God said in His word "For the weapons of our warfare are not carnal but are mighty in God for pulling down of strongholds." (2nd Corinthians 10:4). He warned me "For we do not wrestle against flesh and blood, but against principalities, against powers, against the rulers of the darkness of this age, against spiritual wickedness in heavenly places." (Ephesians 5:12). The word was in me. But I was not using the word. The answer to my bondage was in my belief in the power of the anointing, and faith in the one and only true and living God, the God of the universe that created all things, the God that told me "And we know that all things work together for the good of them that loved the Lord, who are called according to His purpose." (Romans 8:28)

Having a trusting relationship with the Son

My growth in Christ consisted of a great love for praise and worship and no follow through in petitioning the Lord who told me to" ask, and it will be given to you; seek, and you will find; knock, and it will be opened to you (Luke 11:9). Some scholars have stated that we need not petition because our Father already knows. With me, God was developing in me a thirst for a relationship with Him. I knew His word, but didn't know Him personally. His word had already promised "as His divine power has given to us all things that pertain to life and Godliness." (2nd Peter 1:3) What made petitioning so hard for me? It wasn't the petitioning that was hard. It was seeking the heart and character of the one that I couldn't see, through an intimate relationship.

Developing a relationship with God, included spending time in prayer, praising Him for His good works, worshipping Him in the Spirit, requesting His guidance, learning about His unconditional love, accepting His encouragement, accepting and requesting His provision, acknowledging His faithfulness, and sharing His word of Hope to the lost.

The development of a relationship with God is key to any prayer request. We must get to know Him and His sovereignty. There has to be a relationship. You cannot be confident in any good relationship without trust. So therein was another key, the trust. God had told me that, "I could trust in Him with all my heart and lean not on my own understanding, in all my ways acknowledge Him and He would direct our paths (Proverbs 3:5-6)

In the Garden

A relationship with the Lord is now everything to me. I acknowledge Him with every breath that I take. I seek His guidance for my situations. I look for Him to take care of me and fulfill His promise to me that He would open the doors that no man can shut (Isaiah 22:22). My bondage is broken predicated on the relationship that I have with God. And now when I cry out to the Lord I know "He has inclined His ear to me." (Psalms 116:2) I became free because of the time I spent with Him as He revealed to me, healed me,.and delivered me.

Arising to meet the Son

As I arose to meet the anointed one, I began to experience Him daily. And for all the things that I had experienced in my Garden I now knew it was time for me to walk in wisdom and the knowledge of Christ.

From the depths of my spirit I had come to recognize that there will never be any other God of my life. There is none other before Him, no other greater that Him, none other to guide me in the spirit of Love. None other to know as much about me, and Love me as much, as He.

He alone had my best interest at heart. Only He sits on the throne, worthy of the praise, glory, and honor for His faithfulness to me. To him will I sing praises, and exalt over every situation. He alone promised to " hide me under the shadow of His wing" (Psalms 17:8), be the author and finisher of my faith (Hebrews 12:2), "be my rock" (Deuteronomy 32:4), and my shepherd (John 10:11). He is all of this to me because of the life, death, and resurrection of the anointed one Jesus Christ.

In the Garden

The anointed one is our Lord and Savior Jesus Christ. The anointing of God is the power to perform a work for Him, because of His Son, through the Holy Spirit. The work that God placed in me can only be done through the gifts imparted through the Holy Spirit. I could not say no to His gifts. At one time I even denied my gifts from God because of my insecurity of the movement of the Holy Spirit—but not anymore. I have the comforter as I experience God in deeper levels, at various realms in the spirit. The Holy Spirit is real.

The word of God says, "For the wages of sin is death, but the Gifts of God is eternal life." (Romans 6:23). The word of God told me that "In His presence there is fullness of Joy, and at His right hand there are pleasures forever more. The word of God tells everyone who reads 2nd Corinthians 3:17 that, "Where the Spirit of the Lord is, is there is Liberty." I am now free to trust, believe, and speak his word that is manifested through utterance.

Revelation

After years of going in a seemingly endless circle, it all began to make sense while I was in the Garden. God was working on me. It was in the Garden that I began submitting more and more of my life to God. And, that is when the Son arose within me. God exposed me, answered questions, and healed me. In the Garden, I became God-dependent. He lifted me to rise up to meet His Son, and catch the rays of deliverance.

While Jesus was in the Garden of Gethsamane He asked His Father to let His cup pass. God in His sovereignty didn't let His cup pass, but He gave Him strength to endure the cross. This is what He did for me in my garden, and what He can do for you.

Thank you God for these completed works! Blessed be the name of the Lord!

In the Garden

1. Have you looked at what God has developed you into? _____

_____

_____

2. As God's flower what is your posture. Are you leaning on Him? _____

_____

3. Do you hear God calling you? What is He saying? _____

_____

4. He has a gift for you. Read Ephesians 4:11-13. Begin to pray and ask God to entrust you with the knowledge of the gift He has for you, how to use it, and when to use it.

_____

_____

5. Has there been a time when God has put a desire of your heart on hold? Describe the situation and how God revealed to you that His timing to release your desire was perfect. _____

_____

6. Do you see God revealing areas of deliverance to you from deeply buried strongholds?

_____

_____

Prayer: *Wise God. How excellent is your name. Thank you for allowing me to rise up to meet your son in the Garden. Thy kingdom come, thy will be done. Your unconditional love has redeemed me. Thank you for every gift you have given me to benefit your people. I honor you for destroying my strongholds. I praise you for delivering me from my inability to trust you, believe in you, and speak your word. Thank you for your working on me in the Garden, and allowing your son to arise within me. All Glory to your name.*

In the Garden

About the Author

Kim Jackson is a member of the Zion Temple Fellowship Church in Baltimore, MD, where she is under the leadership of Bishop J. Charles Carrington, Jr. She serves in the capacity of Director of the Vessels of Honor Singles Ministry, and teaches to the Joshua Generation children's ministry.

Ms. Jackson has a Bachelor of Arts degree in Health Administration from the University of Maryland, Baltimore County. Her 15 years of experience in the health care field, is accentuated by her wealth of experience in the non-profit arena. Her company Wellspring of Living Water, Inc. specializes in assisting in the development of churches through grant writing, program development, and organizational development. Kim is currently enrolled in the Masters program at Family Bible Ministries Worldwide.

In the Garden

Ordering Information
Quick Order Form

Postal Orders should be mailed to:

God's Glory Publishing Company
P. O. Box 31502
Catonsville, MD 21207, USA

Send payment in the form of check or money order payable to:

God's Glory Publishing Company

Pricing: $12.00/book

Sales Tax: Please add 5% for books shipped to Maryland addresses

Shipping: U.S. $3.50 1st book,
additional books $2.50
(within the continental U.S.)

For more information please call: (410) 869-0739